numb

Author
Jacqueline Dineen

Consultant
Freddi Freemantle
(ILEA Maths Co-ordinator)

Wayland

Starting Maths

Numbers
Shapes
Weight
Adding
Measuring
Taking Away

Series Editor: Deborah Elliott
Editor: Amanda Earl

First published in 1990 by
Wayland (Publishers) Limited
61 Western Road, Hove,
East Sussex, BN3 1JD, England

British Library Cataloguing in Publication Data
Dineen, Jacqueline
Numbers.
1. Numbers
I. Title II. Series
513'.2

HARDBACK ISBN 1-85210-845-2

PAPERBACK ISBN 0-7502-0582-2

Typeset by Nicola Taylor, Wayland
Printed by Rotolito Lombarda S.p.A., Italy
Bound by Casterman S.A., Belgium

All the words that appear in **bold** are explained in the glossary on page 30.

Contents

Numbers are everywhere 4
Numbers in the street 6
Numbers on buses and cars 8
Telephone numbers 10
Numbers and time 12
Numbers used in measuring 14
Counting 16
Writing numbers 18
Adding 20
Taking away 22
Multiplying 24
Dividing 26
Using numbers 28
Glossary 30
Books to read 31
Index 32

Can you see the numbers in this picture?
Why do you think they are there?
The runners are wearing numbers so that everyone can see who they are.

There are numbers everywhere.

Look for numbers around you.
Where are they?
What do you think it would be like without numbers?

Make a drawing of your own favourite number and decorate it with shapes and colours.

Why is there a number by this door?

It tells people the number of the house.

Is it the same as your door number?
The number of a house is part of the **address.**
What would happen if we did not have door numbers?

There are other numbers in a street.
Count how many you can spot on the way to school.
Look on signs and in shop windows.
Where else did you find numbers?

Find some magazines and see if you can find pictures of things with numbers on them. Cut out the pictures.
Stick them on to a sheet of paper to make a number picture.

Why do you think there are numbers on buses and cars?

The big numbers at the back of these buses are the route numbers.

What does this tell passengers?
What do you think the other numbers mean.

Can you draw a picture of your family car? Put the **car number plate** in the right place.

How are numbers used inside a car or bus? You will find these **instruments** on the **dashboard**.

Look at all the numbers on a telephone. Could we use telephones without numbers?

There are millions of telephones in the world.
Each one has its own number.

You can't telephone people if you do not know their number.

Your phone number is one of your special numbers.

Have you any other special numbers?

When is your birthday? How old are you? Those are all your special numbers.

Make a birthday list of your friends or family. Write down how old they are.

This busy station is full of important numbers.
What do these numbers mean?

They tell people the time of trains.

We use numbers to count the minutes and hours in the day.
They tell us the time.
Why do we need to know the time?

Can you think of other numbers in your day?
Do you know the date today?
The days of the month are counted in numbers.

Numbers are used on money. They tell us its value.

Lots of games also use numbers, like 'Snakes and Ladders'.
Can you think of any more?

What do these numbers mean?

They are used for measuring weight.

Clare knows how many oranges to put in the marmalade she is making.
She measures out the right amount on the scales.

Numbers are also used to measure length, height and distance.

What size shoes do you take?
Find out what size shoes everyone in your family takes.
Draw round their shoes on a piece of paper.
Who has the longest feet?

Can you count?

These boys are counting on an abacus.

They count the beads and slide them along the wire.

Have you counted on an abacus?
How does it help you?

We use lots of things to help us count – building bricks, our fingers and even **calculators**.
How far can you count?

Do you know the story of Snow White?
Which of the two pictures has the right number of dwarfs in it?
How many dwarfs are there in the other picture?

How many cats are there in this picture?

Point to the right number.
0 1 2 3 4 5 6 7 8 9 10

We have to know how to read and write numbers.
Can you count things and write down the numbers?
Here is a story about greedy monsters.
Find a piece of paper.
Look at the picture and on your paper fill in the question marks.

? greedy monsters lived in a cave.
One day the first monster ate ? bananas.
The second monster ate ? plates of spaghetti.
The third monster came home too late. He had no tea. There was nothing left!

The customer chooses some food. How much will it cost?
The salesperson adds up the food.
She tells the customer how much money to pay.

Adding is a quick way of counting how many things there are altogether.

Use beads or counters to help you add up.
Mrs Brown had 3 hens. She bought 4 more.

How many hens does she have altogether?
You can draw your own number sentence like this one.

You can also write a sum about this 3 + 4.

Can you add up 4 + 3?
What does this tell you?

How many biscuits has Camilla eaten?
Her mum can work it out.
She put 8 biscuits on the plate. How many are left?
This tells her how many Camilla has eaten. How?

A sum like this is called taking away.

How is it useful?
It tells us how many are left.

Karen gets some money for her birthday.
She wants to buy 2 toys.
Taking away helps Karen to find out if she has enough money.

She has 5 coins. One toy costs 2 coins.
How much will she have left?
You can write a sum
5 – 2.
The other toy costs 4 coins.

Has Karen enough to buy both toys?

How many people are playing tennis?

There are 2 players.

How many players in 2 tennis matches?
How many in 4 tennis matches?
You can count up all the players.

Another way is to multiply.
Multiplying is a quick way of adding up equal groups.

You know that there are 2 players each time.
For 2 tennis matches there are 2 groups of 2. 2 + 2
For 4 tennis matches there are 4 groups of 2. 2+2+2+2

How many players in 5 tennis matches?

These children are choosing 2 teams.

How many children will there be in each team?

How can you tell?

You put the same number of children in each team.
You share them into 2 equal groups.
This is called dividing.

Debbie, Simon and Camilla have 6 apples altogether.
How many will they have each. Use beads to help you. Share 6 beads into 3 equal groups.

What would we do without numbers?

We would not know how many children there were in the picture opposite.

You would not know how old you are.
You would not know your birthday.
No one could telephone you.

We have seen many ways of using numbers. Can you think of any more? Look for **digital numbers** too, like the one in the picture, on watches, on televisions and on alarm clock radios.

Make separate number collections – prices, bus numbers, telephone numbers.
Then, make your own numbers book.

Glossary

Address The house or flat number, street name and town where you live.

Calculators Small electronic machines that can be used to do sums.

Car number plate The special number given to each car, which is displayed on plates at the front and back of the car, usually just above the bumper.

Dashboard The panel in a car, in front of the driver's seat, which displays the car instruments (see below).

Digital numbers The special type of numbers seen on electronic machines such as calculators, alarm clock radios and some watches.

Instruments Clock-like dials which help a driver to measure, for example, how fast he or she is going and how much petrol is in the car.

Route A set way (by road) of getting from one place to another.

Books to Read

A Fun Book of Counting, Neil Morris and Peter Stevenson (Firefly, 1990).

A Fun Book of Time, Neil Morris and Peter Stevenson (Firefly, 1990).

Building Maths, Leslie Foster (Macdonald, 1986).

Counting, Pluckrose and Fairclough (Franklin Watts, 1988).

Facts and Figures of Numbers, Diagram Group (Longman, 1985).

First Book of Maths, Annabel Thomas and Nigel Langdon (Usborne, 1986).

First Book of Numbers, Angela Wilkes and Claudia Zeff (Usborne, 1982).

Picture acknowledgements

The pictures in this book were supplied by the following: Aquarius 17 (both); Bruce Coleman 5, 10; Chris Fairclough 5, 8, 12, 20; Sally and Richard Greenhill 6, 28; Lesley Howling 9 (above); Christine Osborne 13 (below); Topham 11 (above), 29; Tim Woodcock cover, 7, 11 (below), 13 (above), 14, 15, 16, 19, 22, 26, 27; Zefa 9 (below). The illustrations are by Peter Bull Art.

Index

Abacus 17
Adding 21
Address 7

Beads 17, 21
Birthday list 11

Calculators 17
Car number plates 9

Digital numbers 29
Dividing 27
Door number 7

Height 15
Hours 13

Length 15

Measuring 9, 15
Minutes 13
Money 13, 23

Multiplying 25

Number collections 29
Number picture 7
Number sentence 21

Route number 9

Scales 15
Shoe sizes 15
'Snakes and Ladders' 13
Snow White 17
Special numbers 11
Sums 21

Taking away 23
Telephone numbers 10–11
Time 13

Weight 15